AI CHAIR DESIGN

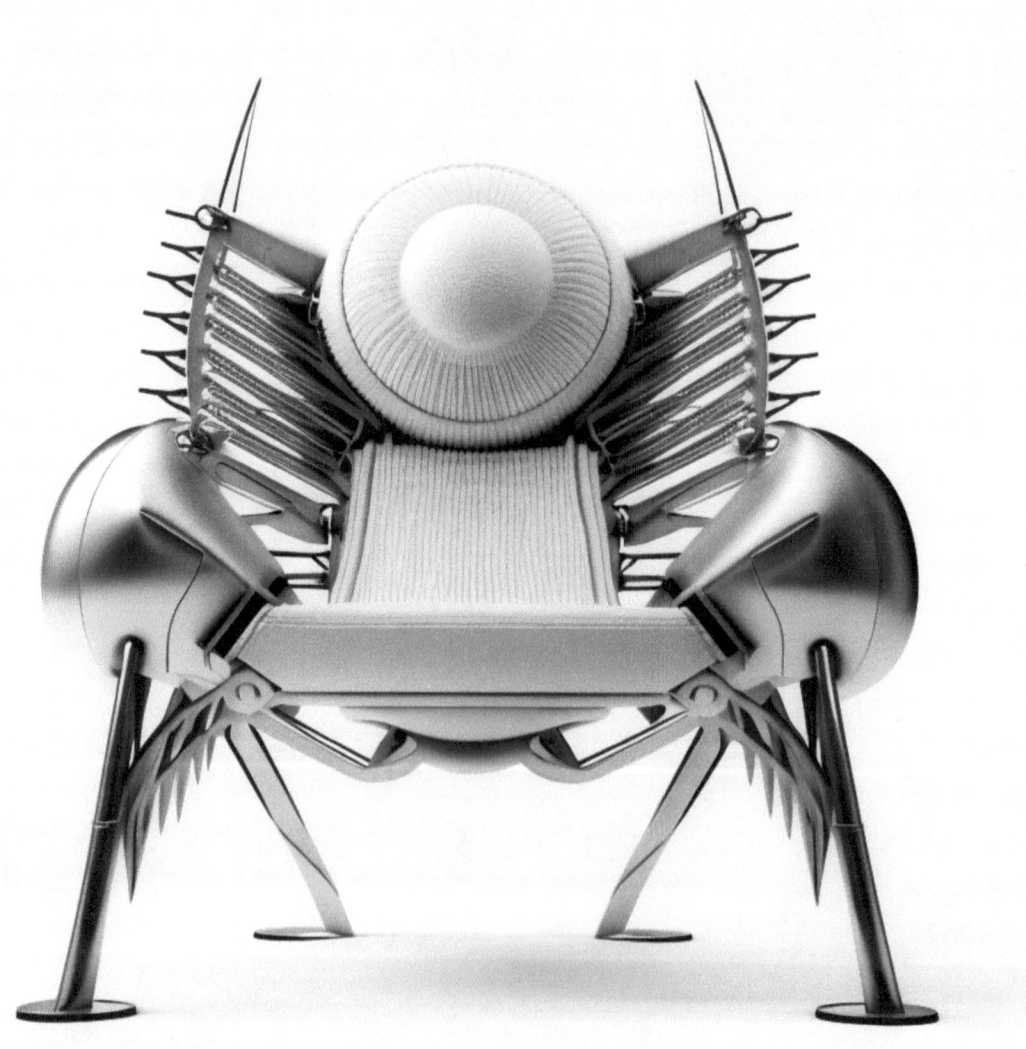

Contents

A Brief History of Chair Design	Page 5, 7
Origin of Generative AI	Page 9
What is Generative AI	Page 11
Generative AI in Design	Page 13
How to Integrate Generative AI	Page 15
Examples of Generative AI	Page 17
Concerns Over GenAI	Page 19
Challenges and Opportunities	Page 21
Choosing Generative Software	Page 23
Design Education	Page 25, 26
Humanities	Page 27
Material Exploration	Page 29, 31
Creating an Image Dataset	Page 33
AI and Traditional Craftsmanship	Page 38 - 41
Prototyping	Page 43
User-Centric Design	Page 45
Watermarking	Page 46
Side Chairs	Page 47
Upscaling	Page 67
Commas	Page 68
Design Criteria	Page 69
Prompt Structure	Page 70

Contents

Carvers	Page	71
How Many Images To Use	Page	88
Image Weights	Page	89
Futuristic	Page	90
Feedback Loops	Page	102
Post-processing	Page	103
Classic	Page	104
Tips and Tricks	Page	120, 121
Something Completely Different	Page	122
In The Style Of	Page	142
Copyright	Page	143
Indemnification	Page	144
Lounge Chairs	Page	145
Sustainability	Page	166
Ecocentric Design	Page	167
Ethics	Page	168
AI Errors	Page	171
Model Training	Page	182, 183
Interactive AI	Page	184, 186
Mutation	Page	188
Anthropomorphism	Page	199, 200
Transparency	Page	201
Conclusion	Page	202
Glossary	Page	204 - 207

A Brief History of Chair Design

Throughout my research into chair history, one quickly discerns the transformative journey of the seemingly mundane chair. It's not merely a matter of carpentry or functionality; the evolution of chair design provides a unique lens through which we can view societal, cultural, and technological shifts.

Ancient Egypt provides some of the earliest recorded chair use and design instances. Contrary to mere functional entities, chairs in this civilization were emblematic of societal ranks. Distinctive designs were reserved for the elite, such as pharaohs and nobles. At the same time, the majority used simpler alternatives like stools or mats.

In ancient Greece and Rome, chairs were symbols of power and prestige used by rulers, magistrates, and priests. Rich in art and culture, these civilizations integrated symbolic power structures into chair design. Animal motifs, from lions to dolphins, were prevalent, underscoring the union of form and symbolism.

The Middle Ages marked a departure from the luxury of earlier eras. During this period, chairs were less common and leaned towards minimalistic designs. They were predominantly the privilege of the clergy and royalty, while benches became standard for the masses.

AI CHAIR DESIGN

A Brief History of Chair Design

In the Renaissance period, with its cultural resurgence, we witnessed an infusion of artistry into chair design. Detailed archival studies and museum collections from the 18th century reveal an affinity for styles like Rococo, Baroque, and Neoclassical. The Industrial Revolution in the 19th century further democratized chair design, making it more accessible to broader segments of the population due to streamlined production processes.

In the 20th century, chair design reached new heights of innovation and creativity. Designers embraced modernism and its simplicity, functionality, and mass production principles. They also explored new materials such as plywood, steel, aluminium, plastic, fiberglass, and foam.

In the 21st century, chair design continues to evolve and challenge the boundaries of form and function. Designers use digital technologies such as computer-aided design (CAD), 3D printing, and artificial intelligence (AI) to create novel, efficient, and diverse chair options that meet various criteria and constraints.

In summation, the historical trajectory of chair design is a rich tapestry of cultural, societal, and technological narratives. As a designer, it's both a privilege and a responsibility to chronicle and analyse this fascinating evolution.

AI CHAIR DESIGN

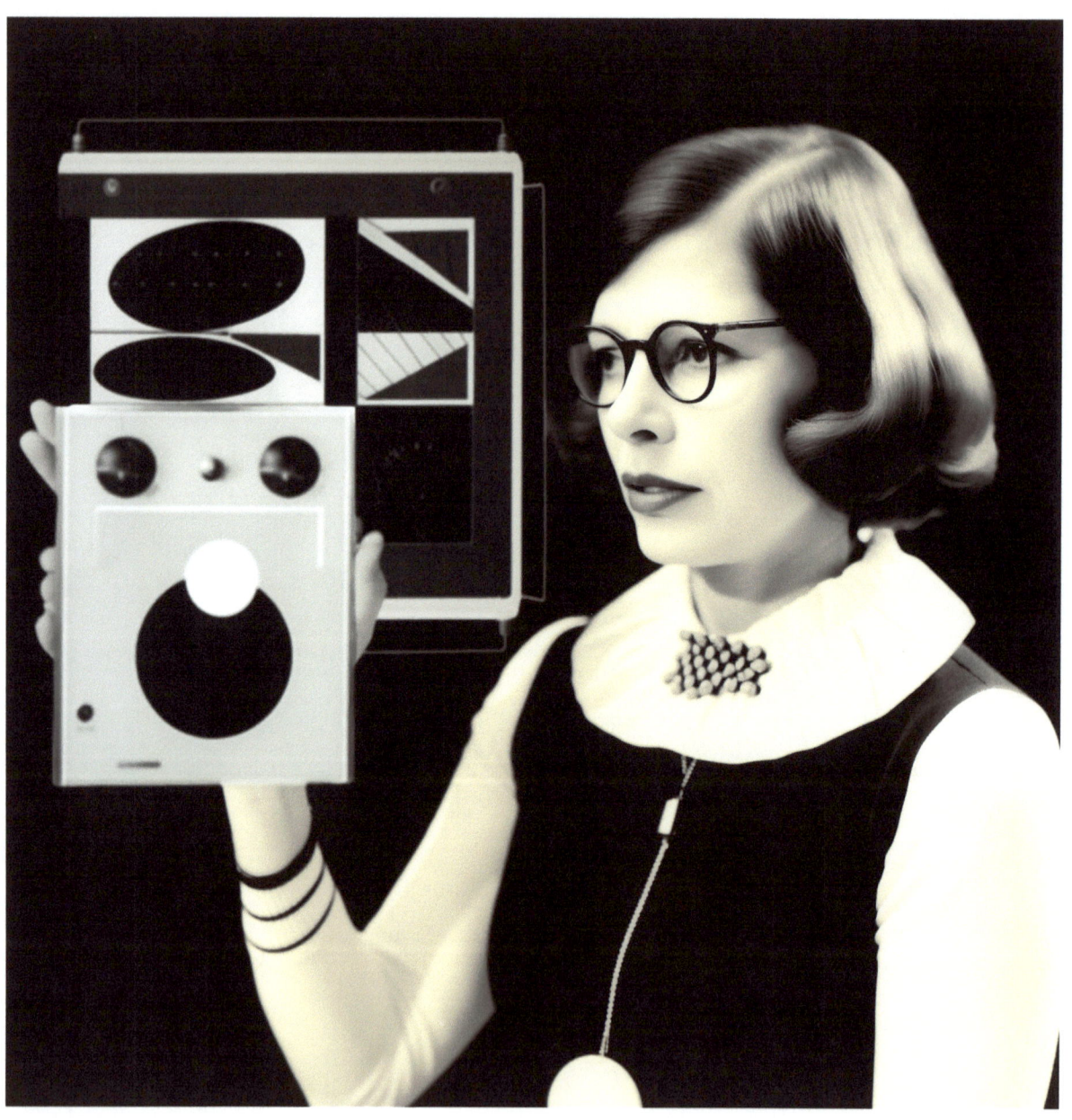

Origin of Generative AI

Generative AI, often abbreviated as GenAI, traces its origins to the mid-20th century, specifically the 1950s. During this era, pioneering computer scientists investigated the potential of algorithms for data generation.

Generative AI uses machine learning algorithms and mathematical models to learn from data and perform complex tasks. During the training phase, these algorithms are fed vast amounts of existing content. They aim to craft new, original output that resembles the training data's characteristics without replicating it.

In more contemporary times, GenAI's prominence and accessibility have surged, a development attributable to the proliferation of expansive datasets, formidable computing capabilities, and the increase in open-source platforms. However, as with many emerging technologies, GenAI has also ushered in a spectrum of ethical and societal difficulties, from concerns about data privacy and intellectual property to issues surrounding misinformation and inherent biases.

AI CHAIR DESIGN

AI CHAIR DESIGN

What is Generative AI

While numerous AI systems are tailored for tasks such as categorizing, identifying, or analysing pre-existing content, like face recognition or language translation, generative AI is engineered to weave new images, textual content, music, and more.

The essence of generative AI lies in its ability to reflect or analyse pre-existing training data and take a bold stride into the domain of creation, embodying a blend of analytical precision and imaginative ingenuity.

As it continues to evolve, generative AI holds a promising potential to redefine the contours of machine-driven creativity, opening novel avenues across a myriad of disciplines. Through generative AI, we stand on the cusp of a new era where machines can contribute to creativity and innovation in ways hitherto unimagined.

AI CHAIR DESIGN

Generative AI in Design

Generative AI platforms offer a range of capabilities that can significantly complement traditional design methods. They can produce many design options and ideas that might not be immediately obvious. This can stimulate creativity and inspire new directions in design work. AI tools can quickly generate visual prototypes and mock-ups, allowing designers to visualize concepts and iterate faster than traditional methods. This rapid prototyping can be especially beneficial in the early stages of design, where multiple iterations might be necessary.

AI platforms can tailor designs to individual preferences or specific requirements. For instance, they can adapt designs to different cultural contexts or personalize them for individual users, which is time-consuming with traditional methods.

In Data-Driven Design, generative AI can incorporate large amounts of data to inform design decisions. This can include user behaviour, market trends, or environmental data, leading to designs more aligned with real-world requirements and user needs.

AI tools can make design more accessible to non-designers, allowing for greater collaboration across disciplines. They can act as a bridge between technical and non-technical team members, facilitating better communication and understanding of design concepts.

AI CHAIR DESIGN

How to integrate Generative AI

Integrating generative AI into a design studio is a forward-thinking move that can significantly enhance creative processes. You will need to familiarize yourself with what generative AI can and cannot do. This includes understanding the types of designs it can generate, the quality of output, and its limitations in creativity and originality.

Consider how generative AI can fit into your existing design workflow. This could involve using AI for initial concept generation, refinement of ideas, or even for creating final design elements. Understand how to combine human creativity with AI capabilities. This involves recognizing when to rely on AI for efficiency and when to prioritize human judgment and creativity.

Don't be afraid to experiment. The best way to understand the potential of AI in your studio is to test it in different scenarios and for various applications. Use feedback loops to improve AI outputs. Educate your clients about the role of AI in your design process. Clear communication about how AI is used, its benefits, and its limitations can set realistic expectations and foster trust.

The quality and diversity of the data used to train the AI will directly impact the quality of its designs. Consider how to source or create diverse data sets that align with your design goals. By focusing on these areas, you can effectively integrate generative AI into your design studio, enhancing creativity, efficiency, and overall output quality.

AI CHAIR DESIGN

Examples of Generative AI

Generative design software is used in various industries to optimize product designs for specific constraints like weight, strength, and material usage. For example, General Motors used this technology to design a new seat bracket that is 40% lighter and 20% stronger than the original part.

In architecture and urban planning, Spacemaker, now part of Autodesk, uses AI to help architects and urban planners optimize the layout of buildings and urban spaces. Spacemaker's AI analyses factors like sunlight, terrain types, and urban regulations to propose the most efficient designs.

In interior design, platforms like Modsy use AI to help users visualize and design their interior spaces. Users upload photos of their space, and Modsy's AI creates a 3D model, suggesting layouts and furniture arrangements.

Each of these examples highlights how generative AI is transforming different areas of design, making processes more efficient, creative, and personalized.

AI CHAIR DESIGN

Concerns Over GenAI

There are concerns that relying on AI for design can diminish the role of human creativity and originality. Critics argue that AI-generated designs might lack the unique touch and deep conceptual thinking a human designer brings. Some fear that AI could replace human designers, leading to job loss in the creative industry. However, others argue that AI will augment rather than replace designers, handling more mundane tasks and leaving complex, creative work to humans. There's also worry that over-reliance on AI tools might lead to degrading traditional design skills, as designers might become too dependent on AI to solve problems.

Another issue is that these tools might not be accessible to all designers, especially those from underprivileged backgrounds or developing countries, due to costs or technological barriers. Introducing AI in design will change the skill set required for designers. Traditional design skills might become less important than skills in guiding and evaluating AI-generated content, which can be a challenging transition for current professionals.

While these arguments present valid concerns, it's also important to note that many in the industry view generative AI as a tool that can significantly enhance the design process and open up new creative possibilities when used responsibly and ethically.

AI CHAIR DESIGN

Challenges and Opportunities

AI generative design presents a mosaic of challenges and opportunities in the contemporary design realm. On the opportunity front, AI stands as a catalyst for designers, enabling them to craft unique, efficient, and diverse product designs that seamlessly dovetail with multifaceted criteria, from aesthetics to sustainability.

However, it has its challenges. AI's susceptibility to echo biases from data sources or inherent algorithmic tendencies can skew the design output, sometimes leading to exclusion or favouritism.

Errors in generative designs can sometimes culminate in impractical or unsafe results. Beyond the operational challenges, AI-driven design beckons questions of ethical, societal, and legal importance, particularly concerning ownership and responsibility.

As the design industry navigates this AI-enhanced era, it faces balancing these opportunities and challenges. Designers must navigate these complexities thoughtfully, leveraging AI's benefits while addressing its limitations and ethical considerations. In this context, the evolution of best practices signifies a transformative period for design thinking, emphasizing the need to maintain creativity, originality, and human connection in design.

AI CHAIR DESIGN

AI CHAIR DESIGN

Choosing Generative Software

I have found that using generative AI can be an exciting and daunting venture. Before diving into the options, clarify what you need from the AI software. Are you focusing on graphic design, 3D modelling, audio production, or something else? Different tools excel in different areas. Look into the most popular and highly-rated generative AI software. Read reviews, check user feedback, and explore case studies or examples of work created with these tools. Some AI software might have plug-ins or extensions for popular design programs.

A strong user community and good customer support can be invaluable, especially starting out. Check if there are active forums, tutorials, and customer service support. Before committing to a purchase, see if a trial version or demo is available.

Generative AI software can range from free to expensive. Consider your budget and the value the software provides. Sometimes, more expensive software offers more features that may be worth the investment in the long run. Understand how the software handles data and its stance on ethical concerns.

Don't be afraid to experiment with different tools. The best way to learn is by doing. I've found certain software to be more intuitive or effective for my work style than others. Remember, the "best" software often depends on your needs, preferences, and work type. It's worth taking the time to explore and find the right fit for you.

AI CHAIR DESIGN

Design Education

The advent of the AI-enhanced design era will inevitably reshape design education and training. Educators and institutions must adapt their curricula and teaching methodologies to prepare future designers effectively.

Design programs will likely incorporate courses specifically focused on AI and machine learning. These courses would cover the basics of AI, machine learning principles, data analysis, and how these tools can be applied in design.

Students will learn how to collaborate with AI as a design partner. This includes understanding how to input ideas into AI systems effectively, interpret AI-generated designs, and refine these outputs to meet specific design goals.

With AI handling more technical design aspects, education will likely emphasize creativity, conceptual thinking, and human-centred design. Students will be trained to think critically and creatively about design problems, positioning them to use AI as a tool rather than a crutch.

Design Education

Practical, hands-on experience with AI design tools and software will be essential. This includes training in 3D modelling software, generative design tools, and other AI-assisted design platforms. As AI takes over more technical tasks, soft skills like communication, collaboration, and adaptability will become more important. Designers must be adept at presenting their ideas, working in teams, and adapting to new technologies and methodologies. AI can significantly aid in sustainable design and assessing social impact. Education will likely emphasize using AI to create ecocentric, socially responsible designs.

AI is rapidly evolving, so designers must commit to lifelong learning. Educational programs might emphasize teaching students how to stay updated with emerging technologies and trends.

More emphasis will need to be placed on project-based learning, where students tackle real-world problems using AI tools. This approach would provide practical experience and better prepare students for industry challenges.

Overall, design education in the AI-enhanced era will be more dynamic, interdisciplinary, and focused on balancing technical skills with creativity, critical thinking, and ethical considerations. This evolution will prepare future designers to use AI effectively, innovate, and lead in an AI-integrated design landscape.

Humanities

Teaching humanities to future design students is essential for their engagement with generative AI. A thorough grasp of art, design history, and philosophy provides a window into earlier creative practices, styles, and breakthroughs. Such understanding fuels students' creativity when using AI, encouraging them to explore new frontiers while honouring past achievements. It cultivates an aesthetic awareness vital for creating functional, visually pleasing, and emotionally resonant products.

Learning about historical design solutions empowers design students to tackle contemporary challenges related to AI with innovative thinking. Delving into philosophy, history, and creative methods prepares them to infuse generative AI with a human-centric view, ensuring it aligns with human values and goals instead of undermining them.

Furthermore, a humanities education nurtures empathy, an indispensable trait for designers. Comprehending a variety of human experiences and viewpoints is key to developing AI technologies centered around users, making them more accessible, inclusive, and beneficial for a diverse population. Focusing on people, ethics, culture, and the understanding of knowledge, a humanities education equips design students to use generative AI in thoughtful, inclusive, and enriching ways. Despite technological advancements, the human aspect remains irreplaceable.

AI CHAIR DESIGN

Material Exploration

Generative AI platforms, such as those developed by companies like Google DeepMind, are increasingly used for material exploration and innovation, a field with immense potential for designers. The DeepMind database, 'Materials Project', provides open web-based access to known and predicted materials and powerful analysis tools to inspire and design novel materials.

AI algorithms can predict the properties and behaviours' of new materials before they are physically created. Using vast datasets on existing materials, AI can model how different combinations of elements might perform, saving time and resources in the material development process. AI can rapidly analyse and screen thousands of material combinations to identify those with desirable properties. This process, which would take much time manually, can be accomplished with AI in a fraction of the time.

AI can delve into the molecular structure of materials, understanding and predicting how changes at the molecular level can affect the material's overall properties. It can optimize materials for specific purposes by tweaking their compositions.

These platforms enable virtual simulations of how materials will perform under various conditions. This allows for extensive testing without needing physical prototypes, which is cost-effective and faster.

AI CHAIR DESIGN

Material Exploration

Designers will have access to a broader range of innovative materials tailored for specific applications, opening new avenues in product and furniture design. AI will help identify more sustainable materials by being more durable, recyclable, or have less environmental impact in their production and disposal. Designers can request materials with specific properties suited to unique design challenges, leading to more customized and effective product solutions.

AI is helping to develop materials that can repair themselves when damaged, which will be revolutionary for products that undergo wear and tear. Materials that change properties in response to external stimuli (like temperature or pressure) will be refined using AI, leading to adaptive and responsive designs. Developing new, environmentally friendly materials will be accelerated with AI, aiding the fight against pollution and waste.

In conclusion, using generative AI in material exploration and innovation opens up many exciting possibilities for designers. It equips them with a broader array of materials and ensures they are more sustainable, efficient, and suited to specific design needs. The potential for discovering novel solutions that address current material limitations is vast, and this advancement is poised to revolutionize the design field.

AI CHAIR DESIGN

Creating an Image Dataset

The nature of your project, whether it's generating faces, landscapes, or objects, will dictate the kind of images you collect. You'll need diverse images representing all the variations you want your model to generate.

There's no magic number of images to collect for your dataset; however, the larger the set, the more variation you can provide. It's often a balance between providing enough information for the AI to understand the design intent without overwhelming it with conflicting inputs. Usually, starting with 10-20 images is a practical approach, allowing for clarity and a focused design direction.

In the first dataset I made, I used images of chairs I produced and rendered images of models I drew in CAD (computer-aided design). Pages 34 and 35 show the 'Homemade dataset made up of my own work (keeping me on the right side of copyright law). Pages 36 and 37 show an augmented dataset I made using the 'Homemade' dataset on pages 34 and 35. This is how you build larger datasets with greater variation and more aligned with your personal aesthetic.

AI CHAIR DESIGN

Homemade Dataset

AI CHAIR DESIGN

Homemade Dataset

AI CHAIR DESIGN

Augmented Dataset

AI CHAIR DESIGN

Augmented Dataset

AI CHAIR DESIGN

'Spooky' chair process images

AI CHAIR DESIGN

AI and Traditional Craftsmanship

In an era where technology and tradition converge, the 'Spooky Chair' emerges as a ground-breaking symbol. The chair was conceived using generative AI and brought to life through the meticulous art of traditional woodworking. Unveiled on September 29, 2023, this chair represents a fusion of old and new and a significant leap in design methodology.

The project, by Sami Kallio Studio, explores the integration of AI in design, a journey marked by curiosity and innovation. Employing three publicly available AI apps, the team ventured beyond conventional design boundaries, generating images from text to align with a fictional client's vision.

This process, traditionally involving problem analysis, sketching, and production drawings, now stands transformed by AI's potential. "Understanding and engaging with it is paramount, as we can shape its role and future development. Our focus was to find a concept that challenged us technically, brought something new to the table, and also tied into the DNA of the studio".

AI CHAIR DESIGN

AI CHAIR DESIGN

AI Innovation and Traditional Craftsmanship

"This exploration is more than just about creating a unique piece of furniture; it's an experiment designed to ignite discussions about AI's role in the design industry. It challenges technical limits, brings novel perspectives, and stays true to the studio's essence. The project reflects a belief that AI, like CAD and CNC, will soon become an integral part of the creative journey, transforming everything from ideation to production".

As AI reshapes the design landscape, Sami Kallio Studio emphasizes the need for a deep understanding of the industry's history and market dynamics. This knowledge is crucial to employing AI effectively, ensuring originality, and maintaining quality.

Crafted with care in the studio's workshop, the 'Spooky Chair' stands as a beacon of innovation, blending AI's potential with the timeless art of woodworking. It invites us to reimagine the future of design, where tradition and technology coalesce to create the extraordinary.

AI CHAIR DESIGN

Prototyping

Generative AI for rapid prototyping and experimentation represents a significant shift in design methodologies, offering substantial advantages over traditional methods in terms of time and cost efficiency.

GenAI allows designers, especially those in training, to experiment freely without traditional manufacturing costs and time constraints. Designers can rapidly iterate on ideas by tweaking the inputs and parameters for the AI, allowing for quick exploration of alternatives and refinements. It can easily scale designs up or down, adjust complexity, or modify them for different applications. The systems can quickly adapt to changing design requirements or constraints, maintaining flexibility in the design process.

AI can simulate a design's performance under various conditions, providing valuable insights even before a physical prototype is created. By optimizing designs digitally before physical prototyping, Physical prototypes can be limited to later stages of the design process or for designs that have already been vetted through AI, significantly reducing costs.

In summary, GenAI in rapid prototyping and experimentation opens new avenues for innovation, efficiency, and creativity. It enables designers to quickly explore a vast array of design possibilities, make data-driven decisions, and produce prototypes more cost-effectively, all while pushing the boundaries of traditional design practices.

AI CHAIR DESIGN

User-Centric Design

Generative AI can analyse vast amounts of data on user preferences, behaviours', and feedback. By leveraging this data, designers can create products that closely align with the needs and desires of their target audience. AI algorithms can identify patterns and trends in user data that might not be immediately apparent, allowing for more nuanced and tailored design decisions.

Generative AI can take individual user specifications or preferences and automatically adjust designs to meet these unique requirements. This capability is particularly valuable in furniture design, where ergonomics and personal taste are paramount.

Designers can use AI-driven simulations and modelling to ensure their products are aesthetically pleasing and ergonomically sound. AI can analyse human-body interactions with various designs, helping to create comfortable and healthy products. It can also cater to diverse users, including those with disabilities. AI algorithms can be trained to consider various accessibility requirements, ensuring that products are usable and beneficial for a wider audience.

Watermarking

The importance of watermarking AI-generated content is growing significantly. Watermarks play a crucial role in establishing the identity of the creator or owner of the content. With the increasing prevalence of AI-generated designs, asserting ownership is essential, particularly in an environment where digital content can be easily duplicated and shared without appropriate credit. Watermarking safeguards the designer's intellectual property and helps prevent unauthorized usage or replication of the design.

Major AI companies such as Microsoft, Adobe, OpenAI, Google, and Meta have all pledged to develop watermarking tools. This commitment addresses issues like the spread of counterfeit images and differentiating content created by AI.

Watermarks are crucial in licensing agreements for designers looking to monetize their AI-generated work. They help track the usage of designs and enforce licensing terms. For individual creators, there are various user-friendly and efficient software options for watermarking, including Adobe Photoshop, Watermark Software, and Canva. As AI technology evolves and its application in design broadens, watermarking's role in protecting creators' and consumers' rights and interests is expected to become even more significant.

AI CHAIR DESIGN

SIDE CHAIRS

SIDE CHAIRS

AI CHAIR DESIGN

SIDE CHAIRS

AI CHAIR DESIGN

SIDE CHAIRS

AI CHAIR DESIGN

SIDE CHAIRS

AI CHAIR DESIGN

SIDE CHAIRS

AI CHAIR DESIGN

SIDE CHAIRS

AI CHAIR DESIGN

SIDE CHAIRS

AI CHAIR DESIGN

SIDE CHAIRS

AI CHAIR DESIGN

SIDE CHAIRS

AI CHAIR DESIGN

SIDE CHAIRS

Upscaling

The images showcased in this book are not to be confused with actual photographs. You will see the image quality vary throughout the book. In creating this collection, I intentionally refrained from using the upscaling technique on any images. The primary focus for this compilation has been on innovation rather than solely on image quality.

AI Upscaling can be used to increase the quality of low-resolution images. This process involves stretching a lower-resolution image to a larger size and applying enhancement techniques to improve clarity, detail, and sharpness. Despite its utility, upscaling has drawbacks, particularly in design and digital art. It can lead to loss of detail, the introduction of visual artefacts, and colour balance and contrast alterations. Upscaled images often appear unnaturally digital, lacking the organic qualities of high-resolution originals. In contrast, the advancements in generative AI models over the past year have led to significant improvements in image resolution, detail accuracy, colour fidelity, and overall realism, reflecting the rapid development in the field and its expanding applications in creative and professional domains.

This year, 2023-24, I have spent approximately 2,000 hours collaborating with generative AI, producing roughly 150,000 images. Not all of which were useful.

Commas

Generative AI systems rely on advanced NLP algorithms to interpret prompts. Proper punctuation, such as commas, helps these algorithms parse language more efficiently and accurately. This is because NLP systems often depend on the syntactic structure of sentences, where punctuation plays a crucial role.

Using commas in prompts is essential when working with generative AI software. Commas help break down the prompt into distinct elements, making it clearer for the AI to understand each aspect. This leads to more accurate and relevant image generation, particularly in complex prompts that require managing multiple details. By separating different visual elements, themes, or actions, designers can influence the final image more effectively.

By clearly separating different concepts or elements, designers can easily modify or rearrange parts of the prompt to achieve different results. This flexibility is particularly useful in iterative design processes where subtle changes in the prompt can lead to significantly different output.

Where multiple designers might contribute to or modify prompts, using commas and consistent punctuation ensures that everyone understands the prompt's structure clearly. Well-structured prompts can also reduce the cognitive load on the user. This makes designing and iterating with generative AI more intuitive and less mentally taxing, especially for complex creations.

Design Criteria

The effective use of generative AI in design hinges on the user's ability to define and communicate design criteria accurately. The more detailed and specific these inputs, such as adjectives, materials, features, size, and colour, the more accurately the AI can generate designs that align with the user's vision. For instance, specifying "a lightweight, durable, red aluminium chair with a modern aesthetic" gives the AI a clear framework.

Well-defined criteria streamline the design process, reducing the time spent on iterations. If the AI understands what is required, it can quickly generate multiple options, saving valuable time and resources in the design process.

Some designs may involve complex requirements that are challenging to conceptualize and execute manually. AI can handle these complexities more effectively if the parameters are clearly defined.

In a rapidly changing market, the ability to quickly generate and iterate designs based on specific and evolving criteria can give companies a competitive edge. This responsiveness is particularly important in industries where trends and consumer preferences change swiftly.

Prompt Structure

A "prompt" refers to the input given to an AI model to generate a response or create content. Begin with a clear and concise statement of what you want when writing a prompt. This helps set the context for the AI. After stating the main request, provide details crucial to your expected output. The more precise you are, the better the AI can tailor its response to your needs.

If you have several important points, list them in a clear, enumerated format. This structure makes it easier for the AI to understand the multiple components of the request. When certain constraints or preferences are important to the task, state these early in the prompt. If the prompt is long or complex, conclude with a summary that encapsulates the critical points. Arrange your instructions in the order that you would logically expect them to be addressed. The AI often processes information sequentially, so the order can influence the output.

Complex language can sometimes introduce ambiguity. You might not get the perfect output on the first try. Be prepared to refine your prompt based on the responses you get, highlighting or rephrasing the important parts as needed.

CARVERS

CARVERS

AI CHAIR DESIGN

CARVERS

AI CHAIR DESIGN

CARVERS

AI CHAIR DESIGN

CARVERS

AI CHAIR DESIGN

AI CHAIR DESIGN

CARVERS

AI CHAIR DESIGN

AI CHAIR DESIGN

CARVERS

AI CHAIR DESIGN

AI CHAIR DESIGN

How Many Images To Use

Understanding the optimal number of images to guide the AI can significantly enhance your experience and outcomes. The number of guiding images largely depends on what you are trying to achieve and how complex your design is. If your design is simple or you're aiming for a specific style, a few strong examples (1-3 images) can be sufficient. For more complex or nuanced designs, you might need more images to adequately convey the elements you want to incorporate.

A smaller set of well-chosen images can guide the AI more effectively than a larger set of less relevant or lower-quality images. If your design goal is more exploratory or creative, diverse images can be beneficial. Using too many images, especially if they are very similar, can lead the AI to overfit. This means it might reproduce elements too closely and not provide enough creative variation. Aim for a balance that gives the AI enough freedom to be creative while still adhering to your design goals.

It's a good idea to experiment with different numbers of images to see how the AI responds. This experimentation can help you understand the capabilities and limitations of the AI model you're using. Pay attention to the outcomes of your initial attempts. If the generated images do not align with your expectations, consider adjusting the number and type of guiding images.

AI CHAIR DESIGN

"Image weights"

The use of image weights in generative AI models, particularly those involved in image generation, serves several important purposes and offers various benefits:

Image weights allow you to specify the degree of influence each input image has on the output. This is particularly useful when you're blending elements from multiple sources. By adjusting the weights, you can determine how prominently features from each input image are represented in the final generated image.

They provide a way to fine-tune the results of the generative process. By adjusting the weights, you can experiment with different balances of features and styles, which can lead to more precise or desirable outcomes.

In some cases, image weights can be used to reduce biases in the generative process. By adjusting weights, you can ensure that certain features or aspects are not overrepresented in the generated images.

In summary, image weights in generative AI models offer enhanced control, flexibility, and precision, enabling users to tailor the generative process to their specific needs and goals. This can lead to more accurate, creative, and effective use of generative AI in image creation.

Futuristic

Adopting a futuristic mindset can push designers to challenge the status quo and think beyond traditional boundaries. It motivates them to envision products that could shape the future rather than merely reflecting current trends.

By focusing on the future, designers can pre-emptively address problems or needs that might arise. GenAI can aid in predicting such needs based on data and then offer design solutions tailored to manage them.

The output can reflect a more forward-looking perspective by feeding the AI system with data on emerging technologies, societal shifts, and design trends. Futuristic products often integrate new materials or technologies. GenAI can be trained on databases of these materials and technologies to suggest innovative combinations or applications.

Using generative AI tools to analyse market trends, designers can identify gaps or niches where a futuristic product might find its audience.

In essence, the term "futuristic" can serve as a north star for product designers, guiding their vision and ensuring that they're leveraging the full potential of generative AI to create products that are not just novel but also meaningful and impactful.

AI CHAIR DESIGN

FUTURISTIC

FUTURISTIC

AI CHAIR DESIGN

FUTURISTIC

AI CHAIR DESIGN

FUTURISTIC

AI CHAIR DESIGN

FUTURISTIC

AI CHAIR DESIGN

FUTURISTIC

AI CHAIR DESIGN

Feedback Loops

Often, it's not just about the number of initial images in your dataset but the generative process. You might start with a couple of images, generate some designs, and then use these new images to refine the output through several iterations.

Augmentation techniques can balance out datasets where some classes are underrepresented. Generating new data synthetically is often less expensive and quicker than collecting new real-world data.

The key is to have a feedback loop where the generative design software's output is evaluated, and the best outcomes are selected. Designers provide feedback on AI-created designs, which the AI then uses to generate improved iterations. This iterative process progressively enhances the design quality, incorporating insights and refinements from each feedback cycle.

In some advanced systems, AI can learn from the feedback to adapt its future design suggestions, becoming more aligned with the designer's preferences or project requirements.

Post-processing

It is an essential step in digital art and design, transforming raw AI outputs into refined, professional-quality works. This process involves various techniques and tools that enhance, correct, and personalize the initial AI creations.

AI-generated designs, while innovative, often come with limitations such as unexpected patterns, abstract elements, or lack of precision. Post-processing addresses these issues, enhancing the design's aesthetic appeal and suitability for the intended purpose.

Post-processing involves techniques such as cleaning up artefacts, enhancing details, colour correction, and resizing. Creative enhancements offer a chance to add personal touches. This can include adding new elements, applying artistic effects, or blending the AI design with traditional media. The process extends beyond correction, allowing artists to infuse their style and vision into the AI-generated base.

Post-processing AI-generated images is a blend of technical skill and creative vision. It refines and personalizes the AI output, bridging the gap between algorithmic creation and human aesthetic sensibilities.

AI CHAIR DESIGN

CLASSIC

AI CHAIR DESIGN

CLASSIC

AI CHAIR DESIGN

CLASSIC

AI CHAIR DESIGN

CLASSIC

AI CHAIR DESIGN

CLASSIC

AI CHAIR DESIGN

CLASSIC

AI CHAIR DESIGN

CLASSIC

AI CHAIR DESIGN

CLASSIC

AI CHAIR DESIGN

AI CHAIR DESIGN

Tips & Tricks

Outpainting is a process where a generative AI system extends the boundaries of an image by adding new content consistent with the image beyond its original borders. It might involve creating more of a landscape, extending a pattern, or imagining what the rest of a scene might look like based on what is already visible. Outpainting has various applications, including creating panoramic views, designing patterns that require repetition or continuation, and artistic purposes where one may want to extend a painting or drawing.

Generative AI relies heavily on the input text to determine the output image. Spelling mistakes, words smooshed together, or missing space between words could lead to unexpected or irrelevant results because the model cannot understand individual words or phrases. However, In some cases, the AI might create an image that, while not what was intended, could be interesting or artistic in its own right due to the unpredicted interpretation of the prompt. This doesn't work well with furniture design but can be a handy tool for artistic imagery. This is another way of adding mutation to your prompt, which can produce serendipitous results.

AI CHAIR DESIGN

Tips & Tricks

If you're unsure how to write a prompt for an idea and have a picture representing it, you have a helpful function available on Midjourney called '/describe.' The /describe command allows you to upload an image and generate four text prompts based on that image. However, the generated text prompts you get from /describe won't recreate an uploaded image exactly. Still, it will allow you to explore ways to create whatever is in your image.

I have found different combinations of prompts suit different projects. Please try using all three styles to determine which works best for your task.

Text-Only Prompts: AI uses the description to generate or modify content (like creating an image) based on the instructions provided.

Image-Only Prompts: AI modifies or interprets an existing image without additional text instructions, so the AI might enhance it, stylize it, or make alterations based on its training.

Combination Prompts: AI uses an image and accompanying text to generate or modify content according to the text instructions. The most common type of prompt used but only sometimes the most useful.

Something Completely Different

GenAI unlocks a vast array of opportunities across various creative domains. It democratizes creativity, enabling those without formal artistic backgrounds or those with disabilities to venture into mediums previously beyond their reach.

This book is a perfect example of how generative AI can assist people in creating work that wouldn't have been possible without its help. I was diagnosed with ADHD/Autism as a small boy. I firmly believe I owe much of my creativity and drive to my condition; however, writing a book would have been very difficult without the capabilities of AI to help.

When I first delved into GenAI, I explored a spectrum of domains, including fashion, postures, and dynamic movement within the images. The ensuing visuals capture my continuing exploration.

AI CHAIR DESIGN

SOMETHING COMPLETELY DIFFERENT

SOMETHING DIFFERENT

AI DESIGN

SOMETHING DIFFERENT

AI DESIGN

SOMETHING DIFFERENT

SOMETHING DIFFERENT

AI DESIGN

SOMETHING DIFFERENT

AI DESIGN

SOMETHING DIFFERENT

SOMETHING DIFFERENT

SOMETHING DIFFERENT

SOMETHING DIFFERENT

In the Style Of

The phrase "in the style of" when used with generative AI software like Stable Diffusion, Midjourney, or Dall-E is significant, especially in copyright concerns. It refers to creating an artwork that mimics the style of a specific artist or art movement.

When AI generates images "in the style of" a particular artist, the software attempts to replicate that artist's work's unique visual characteristics and techniques. If the artist is still living or their work is still under copyright, creating new works that closely imitate their style could infringe on their copyright. This is because the law protects not just specific works but also the distinctive expression of the artist, which may include their style.

My advice is not to use other people's styles and images and to work solely from your own images or the work you generate (Augmented data). Use period styles like Mid-Century, Rococo, Baroque, or Renaissance to avoid copyright grey areas if necessary. However, it should be remembered that designers who don't use GenAI today regularly take influence and copy the styles of previous designers; this isn't a new problem in design. Careful consideration and respect for copyright laws and artistic integrity are crucial when using these tools.

Copyright

Generative AI operates by processing extensive data archives to generate new creations. This process, while technologically advanced, poses critical questions about copyright infringement. The use of large data sets, often comprising unlicensed works, has led to legal challenges, as seen in cases like Andersen v. Stability AI. Such lawsuits question the ethics and legality of using artists' works without permission to train AI systems. They delve into the heart of copyright law, challenging our understanding of what constitutes a "derivative work" and the application of the fair use doctrine.

The implications of these legal battles extend beyond the realm of AI developers to the users of these technologies, including businesses and individual creators. For instance, Getty's lawsuit against the creators of Stable Diffusion highlights the risks of using copyrighted images without proper authorization. These cases are not just about the legality of AI-generated works but also about the responsibility of AI developers in sourcing their training data.

As the legal landscape evolves, it is imperative for those engaging with generative AI to understand and navigate these complexities. Businesses must scrutinize their contracts and ensure that their use of AI-generated content does not infringe upon existing copyrights. Content creators, too, face the challenge of safeguarding their work against unauthorized use in AI training datasets.

Indemnification

In the realm of AI and technology services, indemnification typically involves the service provider taking on the responsibility to defend their customers in legal disputes related to their services and covering any resulting legal costs or settlements.

Recently, there has been a trend toward leading AI companies offering legal protections to their customers against potential copyright infringement claims, which is a significant development in generative AI. This movement is led by companies like Anthropic, Microsoft, and Google, each taking steps to assure their customers regarding the legal use of their AI-generated content.

These developments reflect an evolving landscape where the legal status of AI-generated content remains a subject of debate and uncertainty. By offering these protections, these companies aim to encourage the use of their generative AI services while addressing customer concerns about potential legal risks. It's a strategy that balances innovation with responsibility, providing a safety net for businesses and individuals exploring the potential of AI in various fields. Always check if your provider offers indemnification against copyright infringement claims.

AI CHAIR DESIGN

LOUNGE CHAIRS

LOUNGE CHAIRS

AI CHAIR DESIGN

LOUNGE CHAIRS

AI CHAIR DESIGN

LOUNGE CHAIRS

AI CHAIR DESIGN

LOUNGE CHAIRS

AI CHAIR DESIGN

LOUNGE CHAIRS

AI CHAIR DESIGN

LOUNGE CHAIRS

AI CHAIR DESIGN

LOUNGE CHAIRS

AI CHAIR DESIGN

LOUNGE CHAIRS

AI CHAIR DESIGN

LOUNGE CHAIRS

AI CHAIR DESIGN

LOUNGE CHAIRS

Sustainability

Generative AI is transforming sustainability in design and production, becoming an essential tool for optimizing resources and enhancing environmental consciousness. It meticulously analyses a product's energy usage, environmental impact, and design fundamentals, pinpointing areas for improvement and proposing effective enhancements.

In industries like construction, manufacturing, and fashion, where material waste is a significant concern, AI algorithms efficiently manage material utilization, thereby reducing waste. This technology also plays a crucial role in minimizing carbon footprints by optimizing energy consumption in production. It smartly schedules operations to coincide with the availability of renewable energy and fine-tunes machinery usage for lower energy consumption.

Moreover, AI facilitates mass customization, creating individually tailored products without the high resource cost usually associated with custom-made items. It leverages extensive datasets to shape design choices, considering environmental, social, and economic sustainability aspects. AI's ability to assess a product's entire lifecycle empowers designers to make more environmentally friendly decisions.

Combining this technology with human creativity offers great promise for a more sustainable future, balancing high-quality and aesthetic standards with ecological responsibility.

Ecocentric Design

Generative AI has the potential to significantly advance the field of ecocentric design, an approach that emphasizes sustainability, environmental friendliness, and harmony with nature. It can analyse vast datasets to identify the most sustainable materials for specific uses and predict the environmental impact of different materials, helping designers make eco-friendly choices.

Generative AI can predict the long-term environmental impact of design decisions, considering factors like climate change, resource scarcity, and ecological trends. This foresight is crucial for making truly sustainable designs in the long run. It can analyse local ecosystems and environmental conditions to tailor designs specifically suited to local climates, flora, and fauna, promoting ecological harmony.

AI can simulate how designs interact with their environment, including factors like wind, water, light, and wildlife. These simulations can lead to designs that are more harmonious with nature and less disruptive to ecosystems. Generative AI acts as a powerful tool for designers committed to ecocentric principles. It enables a more informed, efficient, and innovative approach to designing in harmony with nature, while also addressing the pressing need for sustainability in our world.

Ethics

There's a need for ethical guidelines on sourcing inspiration for AI-generated designs, ensuring respect for cultural heritage and intellectual property. While AI can generate designs based on given parameters, the human touch is essential for injecting emotion, storytelling, and deeper meaning into designs.

There's an ongoing debate about the authenticity and originality of AI-generated designs. Encouraging a symbiotic relationship where human designers refine and contextualize AI-generated ideas will help maintain originality. Designers must make critical decisions about when and how to use AI, ensuring that the final product aligns with ethical standards and social responsibilities. Being transparent about the use of AI in the design process is crucial. This includes disclosing the extent of AI involvement in creating a design.

While GenAI offers remarkable opportunities in the field of design, it's vital to approach its integration with a keen awareness of these ethical implications. Balancing AI's capabilities with human designers' irreplaceable creativity, cultural sensitivity, and ethical considerations will be vital in navigating this evolving landscape.

AI CHAIR DESIGN

169

AI Errors

The quality and accuracy of the AI's outputs depend on the quality and accuracy of the prompts. If the prompts have errors, such as missing spaces between words or images, the generative AI models may produce distorted, incomplete, or irrelevant outputs.

With improper or unclear inputs, the AI is essentially making its best guess, which can result in entirely unexpected results. The best practice is to provide high-quality, well-formatted prompts with precise spacing, terminology, and unambiguous images to AI systems. This allows the AI to interpret the intent accurately and generate the highest quality and most relevant outputs.

In the subsequent images, you'll see the results of different errors in my chair design prompts.

AI CHAIR DESIGN

AI ERRORS

AI ERRORS

AI CHAIR DESIGN

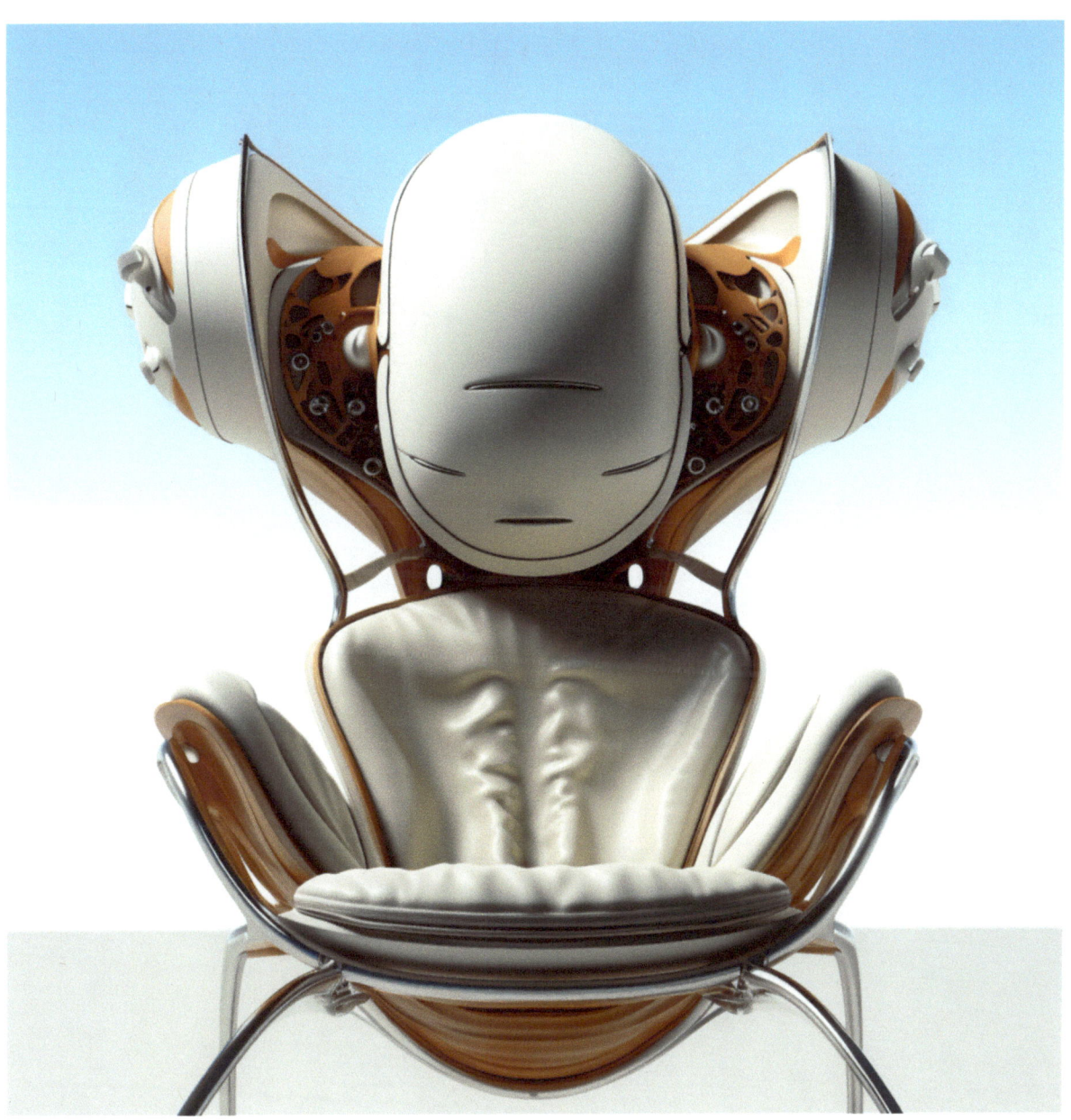

AI ERRORS

AI CHAIR DESIGN

AI ERRORS

AI CHAIR DESIGN

AI ERRORS

AI CHAIR DESIGN

AI ERRORS

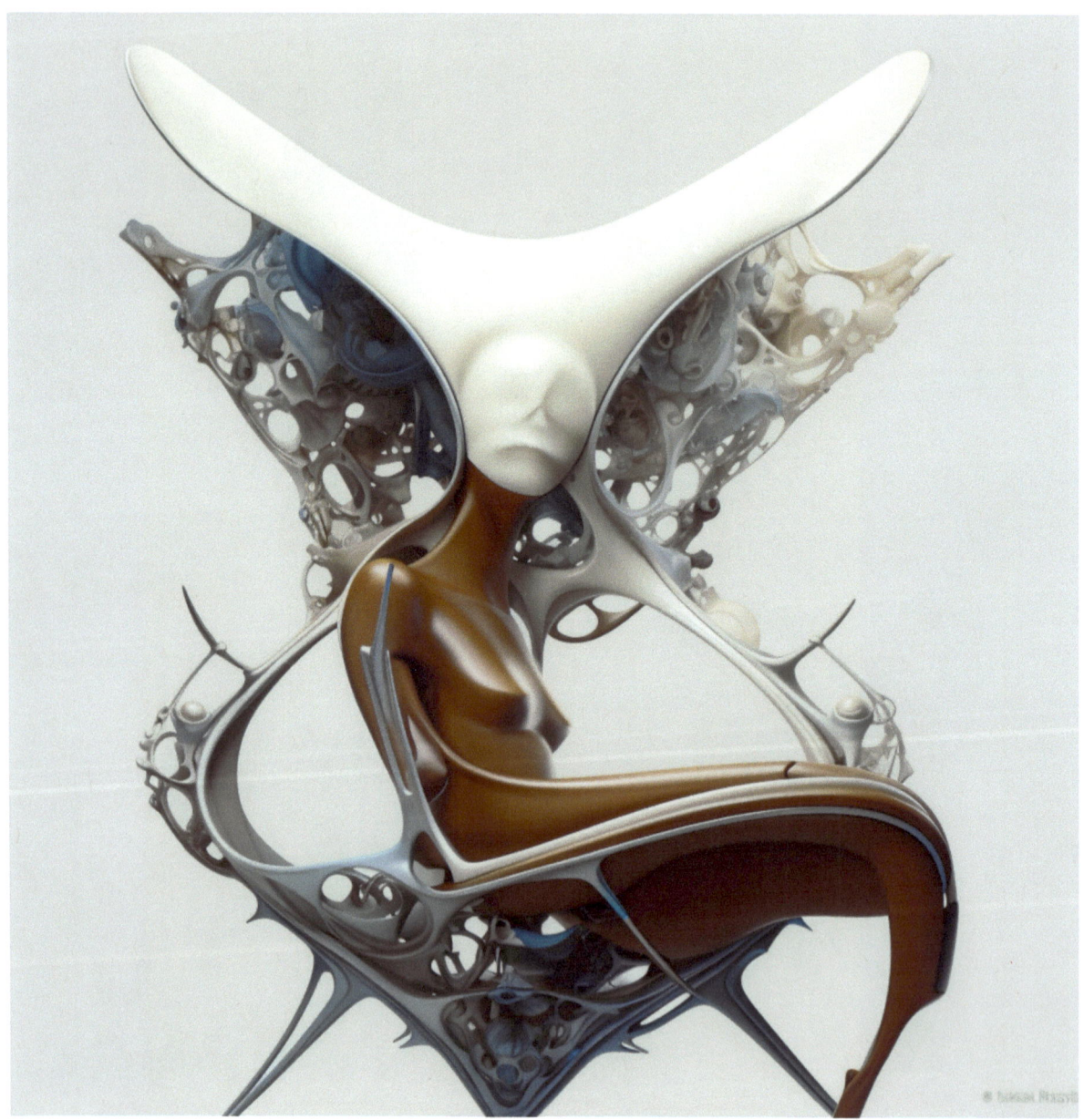

AI CHAIR DESIGN

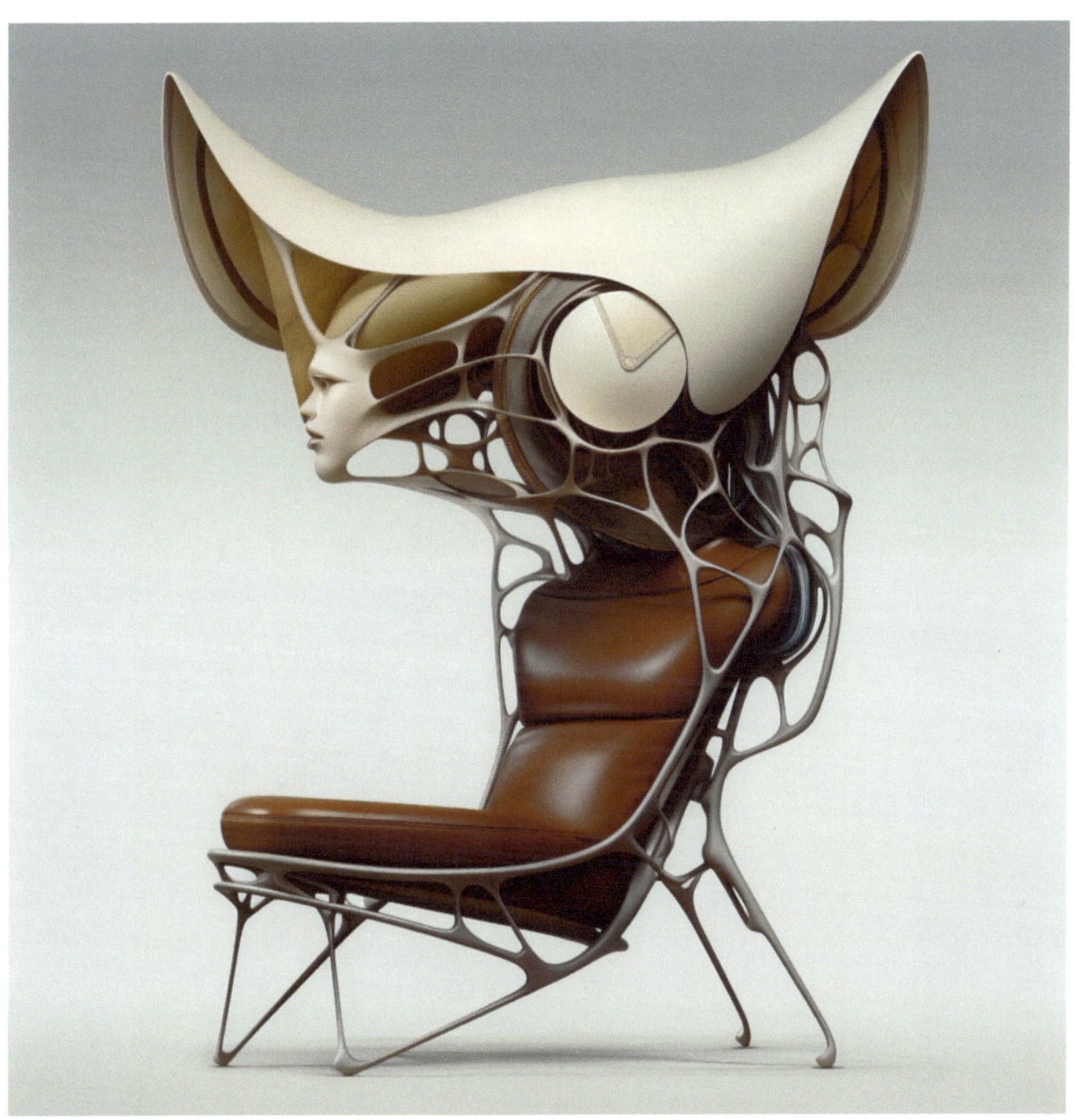

AI ERRORS

Model Training

By training a personal generative AI model, designers and students can tailor them to their specific design needs and preferences. This customization allows the AI to better understand and replicate their unique style, making it more effective in assisting with their specific types of projects.

Training an AI model can be an educational experience for students. It provides hands-on learning about AI, machine learning, and data handling. This understanding can be crucial in a world where these technologies are increasingly important.

A personal AI model can be trained to provide targeted feedback based on the designer's past work and preferences. This can be a powerful tool for continuous learning and improvement, offering personalized critiques and suggestions.

By training their AI on specific datasets, designers can leverage data-driven insights for their projects. This can include material choices, colour schemes, or design trends optimized for their particular market or audience.

By training their own models, designers and students can maintain more control over their intellectual property. This is because the designs generated by the AI are based on their unique input and training data, reducing copyright and design originality issues.

Model Training

Training a generative AI model involves teaching the AI system to understand and create new content similar in style or structure to the training data you provide. Many platforms offer tools for training AI models without needing extensive coding knowledge. Start with simple models and experiments. Use online resources or pre-built models as a starting point, and then gradually move to more complex training as you gain more understanding.

The first step is gathering a large dataset of examples representing the output you want the AI to generate. For a designer, this could be a collection of images, drawings, 3D models, or design patterns they admire or have created themselves.

The collected data is fed into the AI model. This process involves the model analysing the data and attempting to understand the patterns and features that define it. The model iteratively improves its ability to generate similar data. In GANs, for example, one part of the network generates data, and another part evaluates it, in a continuous feedback loop. AI model training is an iterative process. Expect to go through multiple rounds of training, tweaking, and testing the model to improve its outputs. This process requires a basic understanding of AI principles and tools, and a willingness to experiment and learn.

AI CHAIR DESIGN

Interactive AI

As the digital landscape experiences a tectonic shift, we stand at the cusp of a transformation, transitioning from generative AI to the era of interactive AI. This evolution promises to redefine the very fabric of how we interact with technology, particularly for professionals in the design sector.

Generative AI, for all its merits, primarily focuses on crafting content based on the input it receives. It was akin to an advanced tool, ready to follow its user's command. However, interactive AI elevates this dynamic. Rather than simply processing input to create output, this new form of AI understands context, recalls past interactions, and potentially anticipates user needs. This isn't just a minor upgrade; it's a ground-breaking advancement in how humans and machines will communicate.

Consider the life of a modern designer. With generative AI, they'd still be bound by the limitations of manual processes. But with interactive AI, designers could seamlessly toggle between applications using verbal instructions, summon feedback instantly, and even instruct the AI to make design alterations based on market trends. The phrase "time is money" has never been more accurate. With such autonomy in AI, productivity is bound to skyrocket.

AI CHAIR DESIGN

AI CHAIR DESIGN

Interactive AI

The collaborative potential between different AI systems is staggering. Envision a scenario where a content-generating AI liaises with a design-centric AI, crafting a holistic marketing strategy where visuals and text harmonize perfectly.

The newfound agency of interactive AI introduces profound ethical questions. For instance, while a design AI can now autonomously create based on feedback, safeguards must be in place to prevent it from sharing sensitive or proprietary designs. The idea of a "big red button" or an immediate override mechanism isn't just science fiction folklore—it's a genuine necessity in this brave new world.

Moreover, as designers adapt to this transformation, their relationship with AI will metamorphose. No longer will AI be seen as just another tool in their digital arsenal. Instead, it will become a collaborator, a creative partner in the truest sense. This relationship will foster a richer, more dynamic interaction, where ideas bounce back and forth, not between two human minds but between humans and machines.

In essence, the rise of interactive AI isn't merely a technological upgrade—it's a paradigm shift. It signals a future where technology interactions are transactional and conversational. It paves the way for a world where AI doesn't just do as it's told but actively contributes, anticipating needs, offering insights, and enriching the creative process.

AI CHAIR DESIGN

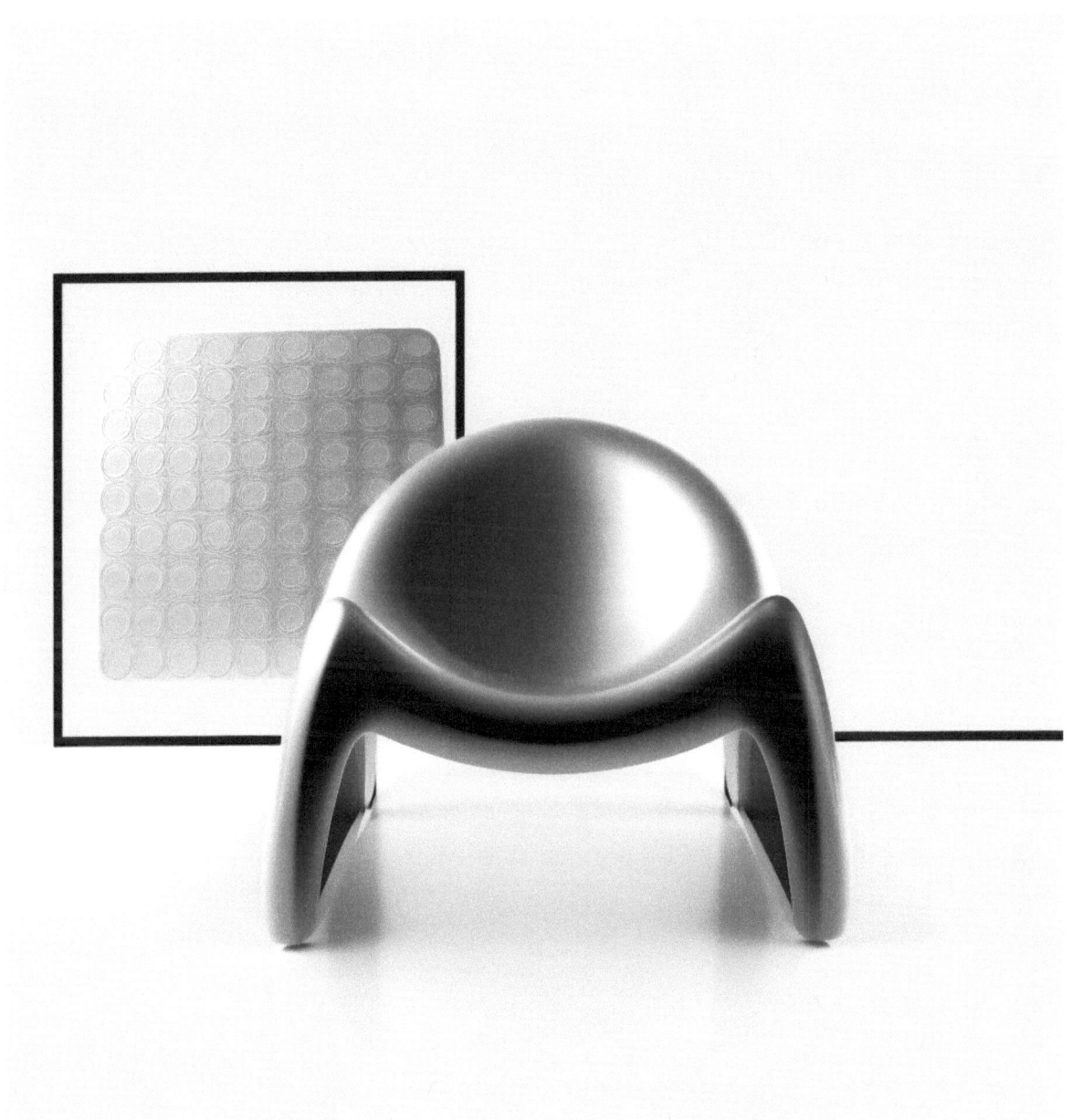

Mutation

During my time at university, I developed a keen interest in genetic algorithms (GAs) and their potential to enhance design optimization in terms of efficiency, durability, and ergonomics.

A pivotal concept within GAs and GenAI is 'mutation,' which introduces random variations to solutions. This is crucial for fostering diversity and averting design stagnation. A delicate equilibrium is maintained through mutation between harnessing current solutions and discovering novel ones. Nonetheless, it's imperative to strike the right balance. Overdoing mutation could yield inconsistent outcomes, whereas insufficient mutation could limit GenAI's innovative potential.

In the subsequent images, you'll see lounge chair designs that used a text prompt that requested a 'lounge chair design,' complemented by a dataset of lounge chairs (5 or so images of chairs I had generated previously that showed potential) and a picture of a butterfly, symbolizing mutation in this context. The final lounge chairs crafted by GenAI represent an amalgamation of these three guiding inputs.

AI CHAIR DESIGN

WING CHAIRS

WING CHAIRS

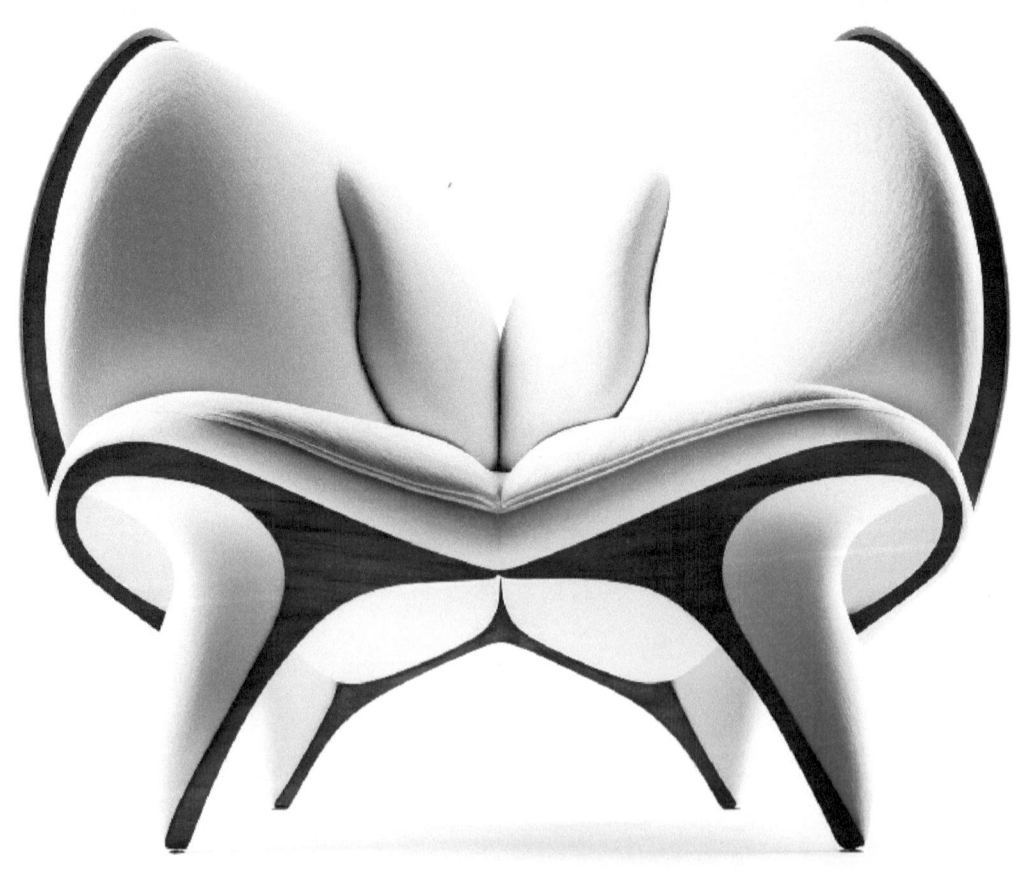

AI CHAIR DESIGN

WING CHAIRS

AI CHAIR DESIGN

WING CHAIRS

AI CHAIR DESIGN

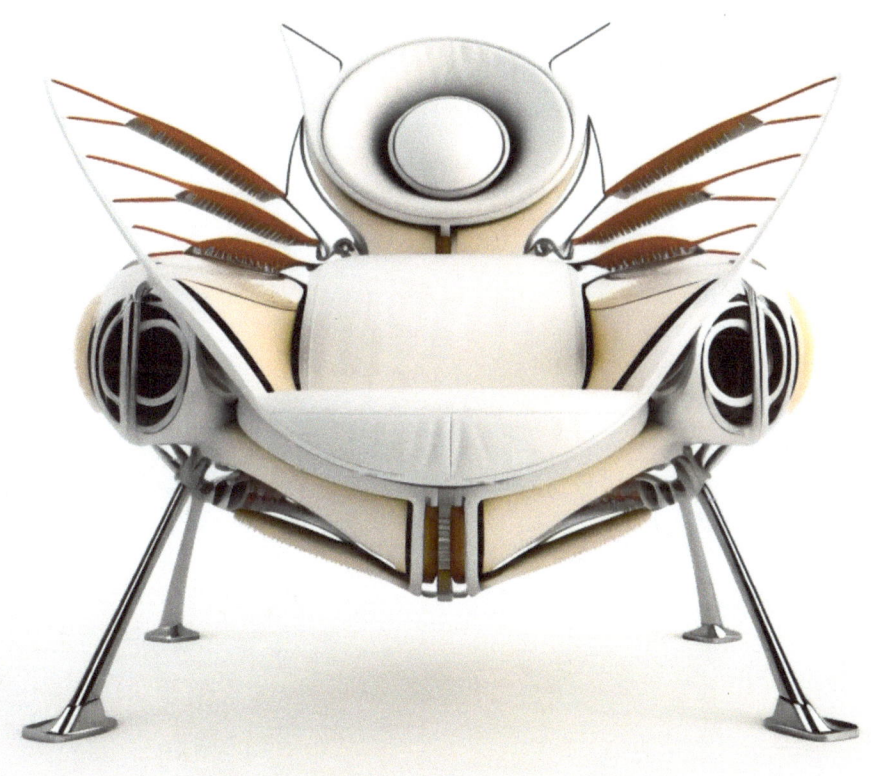

WING CHAIRS

AI CHAIR DESIGN

WING CHAIRS

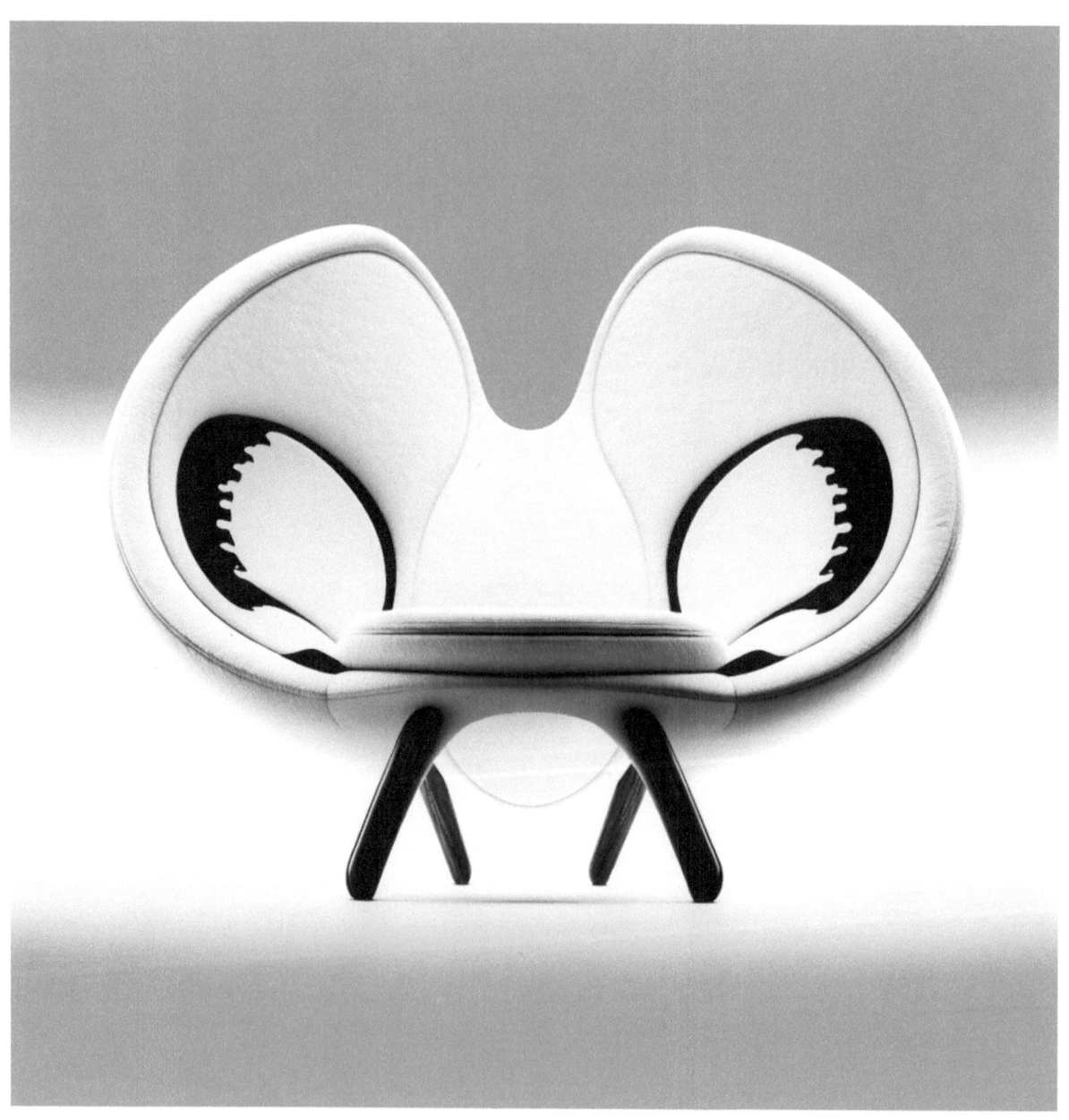

Anthropomorphism

Humans tend to anthropomorphize non-human entities, attributing human-like qualities to them. Developing an emotional attachment to AI systems in the design field is a fascinating prospect as designers and AI grow, work, and evolve together. As AI systems become more interactive and seemingly 'intelligent', designers will start attributing personalities to them.

A relationship where AI contributes ideas and feedback can foster a sense of camaraderie and respect. Over time, AI systems can learn and adapt to individual designers' styles, preferences, and quirks. This means that AI tools would not just be a one-size-fits-all solution but also learn and adjust to complement each designer's unique process. This personalized interaction can create a feeling of being understood and supported.

When a design project the designer and the AI have contributed to succeeds. This shared success reinforces the emotional bond, as the designer may feel gratitude and a sense of team achievement. During challenging phases of a project, the AI can provide support, suggesting solutions and alternatives. Overcoming obstacles together can strengthen the emotional bond, similar to how adversity can strengthen human relationships.

While developing an emotional attachment to AI in the design field is complex and multi-faceted, it is important to approach it with awareness and consideration for the boundaries between technology and humanity. The relationship between designers and AI should ideally enhance human creativity and well-being, rather than replace human connections.

Anthropomorphism

It's essential to educate the public and AI users about what AI is: a tool created by humans, driven by algorithms and data, without consciousness or sentience. This understanding helps prevent the anthropomorphism of AI, which Attributes them to human-like qualities such as consciousness, emotions, and the ability to suffer, which they do not possess.

In media, education, and discourse, it's important to consistently portray AI as a tool or assistant rather than a being. This helps in maintaining a clear distinction between sentient beings and non-sentient tools.

It's vital to understand what AI truly is to make ethical decisions about its development and use. Misunderstanding AI's nature could lead to misplaced priorities and ethical judgments. It's crucial to remember that humans are the creators and operators of AI systems and, thus, fully responsible for their impacts.

Anthropomorphizing AI can lead to fear, mistrust, and resistance against beneficial AI technologies, hindering their adoption and potential positive impacts. A clear understanding of AI's nature encourages responsible innovation, focusing on creating AI systems that are fair, unbiased, and beneficial for society.

AI CHAIR DESIGN

Transparency

In generative design, the clear labelling of AI-generated content is paramount. This transparency fosters trust by openly acknowledging the origin of the content. Ethically, it's essential to prevent the unintentional spread of misinformation, as AI can produce both highly realistic and entirely fictitious outputs.

From a legal and economic standpoint, the lines concerning intellectual property and labour market implications blur when AI generates content. Can AI-produced art be copyrighted, and who then holds these rights? Furthermore, understanding whether a design or piece of art is human or AI-generated can influence its perceived cultural or artistic value.

Moving forward, identifying AI-generated content becomes critical in a digital age teeming with information. Transparency is our anchor as the lines between human and machine-produced content blur. Ensuring audiences can distinguish between these origins is a matter of trust, ethical integrity, cultural value, and informed decision-making.

As AI continues to shape the content production landscape, we must prioritize clarity, ensuring a future where technology complements human creativity rather than obscures it.

Generative AI stands not merely as a tool or an algorithm but as a testament to human ingenuity and our persistent quest for the 'new.' Yet, its power doesn't overshadow the very essence of a human touch. While leaning on the capabilities of GenAI, designers must remember that technology, however advanced, is but an extension of our intellect and not its replacement. The beauty of this symbiosis lies in our ability to marry the computational prowess of machines with the nuanced depth of human creativity.

This narrative has showcased GenAI's expansive possibilities and unveiled its challenges, from echoing biases to legal ramifications. It underscores the need for careful, ethical deployment and an ongoing dialogue about its societal impacts. Moreover, the personal journey interwoven into this exploration affirms the democratizing potential of Generative AI for empowering individuals without a traditional design background; AI becomes an ally, ensuring creativity is an inclusive endeavour.

In the design world, the word 'futuristic' often evokes imagery of sleek innovation. But, as we stand on the brink of this 'AI Enhanced Design Era,' it's imperative to remember that the essence of all future creation lies in the harmonious partnership between man and machine.

Embracing Generative AI is not just about ushering in a technological revolution; it's about envisioning a new era where creativity is amplified, design is democratized, and the future, however futuristic, remains profoundly human.

AI CHAIR DESIGN

Glossary:

3D models: Three-dimensional representations of objects or designs.

Agent-based design: A type of generative design that uses algorithms to model the behavior and interaction of autonomous agents, such as birds, fish, ants, etc., creating emergent patterns and structures from simple rules.

AI Generative Design: An iterative design process that uses a program to generate a variety of designs based on specified parameters.

Algorithm: A set of instructions or rules that a computer follows to solve a problem or perform a task.

Algorithmic tendencies: The patterns or behaviors that algorithms tend to follow based on their design.

Augmented Reality (AR): An interactive experience that overlays digital information, such as visuals or sounds, onto the real world.

Baroque: A 17th-century European style marked by grandeur, emotion, and drama, often seen in architecture, art, and music.

Code generation: A technique in which new code is created based on a given specification, description, or example, using programming languages such as Python, Java, HTML, etc.

Data augmentation: A technique in which additional synthetic data is generated from existing data to increase the size and diversity of the training dataset.

Data sets: Collections of data that are used to train or test AI models, such as images, text, audio, etc. The quality and quantity of data sets can affect the performance and output of generative AI systems.

Deepfake: A type of face swap that creates realistic but fake videos or audio of people saying or doing things they never did, using neural networks to synthesize the facial expressions and voice of the target person.

Design Efficacy: The measure of how effective a design is in achieving its intended purpose or functionality.

Digital Twins: Virtual representations of real-world entities or processes used for various purposes, including testing and optimization.

Echo biases: Repetition or reflection of prejudices, often stemming from the data an AI model was trained on.

Ergonomic Design: A design approach that considers the comfort, efficiency, and safety of the people using the products or systems.

Evolutionary design: A type of generative design that uses algorithms to simulate natural selection and evolution, creating and evaluating multiple variations of a design until an optimal solution is found.

Face swap: A technique that replaces the face of one person with the face of another person in an image or video, using neural networks to align and blend the faces.

Foundation model: A term for large-scale generative AI models that can be used as a basis for various downstream tasks and applications, such as GPT, DALL-E, LaMDA, etc.

Generative Adversarial Network (GAN): A type of neural network that consists of two competing models: a generator that creates new data and a discriminator that evaluates the authenticity of the data.

Generative AI (GenAI): A category of artificial intelligence that focuses on creating new data, which mirrors original input without directly replicating it.

Generative design: A design process that uses algorithms to explore and create multiple possible solutions that meet certain constraints and goals.

Genetic Algorithms (GAs): Search heuristics used to find exact or approximate solutions to optimization and search problems, based on the process of natural selection.

GenAI: Generative AI, often used to denote the broad category of AI systems that produce new content or designs.

Image inpainting: A technique that fills in missing or corrupted parts of an image, using neural networks to infer the plausible content from the surrounding pixels.

Image prompt: A visual command or piece of information input into a system to guide its output.

Image-to-image: A technique that transforms one image into another image, using neural networks to map the input and output domains.

Image-to-image translation: A technique in which an image from one domain is transformed into an image from another domain, such as converting a sketch into a photo or a day scene into a night scene.

Interactive chatbots: Software applications that simulate human conversations and interactions.

L-system: A type of algorithm that uses symbols and rules to generate fractal-like structures, such as plants, trees, snowflakes, etc.

Machine learning: A branch of AI that enables computers to learn from data and experience, without being explicitly programmed.

Neoclassical: A mid-18th to early-19th century movement inspired by the classical art and culture of ancient Greece and Rome, emphasizing clarity, simplicity, and symmetry.

Mutation: A random change in genetic algorithms that introduces variation.

Neural network: A type of machine learning model that consists of layers of interconnected nodes that process and learn from data, inspired by the structure and function of the human brain.

Noise function: A type of algorithm that generates random but smooth values across a domain, such as Perlin noise or simplex noise, creating natural-looking textures and shapes.

Photo-realism: An art style wherein the artist tries to make a painting or digital image look as realistic and true to life as possible.

Procedural generation: A type of generative design that uses algorithms to create complex and varied content from simple rules, such as landscapes, buildings, textures, characters, etc.

Randomness and unpredictability: The element of chance or uncertainty in generative AI outputs, which can lead to unexpected and novel results.

Rococo: An 18th-century artistic style originating in France, characterized by ornate detail, pastel colors, and playful, whimsical themes.

Role of design: The purpose, importance, or influence of design in various contexts, be it artistic, societal, or technological.

StyleGAN: A type of generative adversarial network that specializes in generating images that reflect a specific style.

StyleGAN2: An improved version of StyleGAN, offering better image quality and less artifacts.

My acknowledgements are for:
My wife Zanna, our two children, Saul and Jodie
and my unwavering parents, Keith & Sally
who supported me through every high and low.

"**Disclaimer:** The vast majority of images and text, within this book have been produced in collaboration with Artificial Intelligence (AI) technology." Although the images contained within this book have been generated using AI. I retain sole ownership of the text prompt, seed selections, and results through iteration and final editing.